MAR 14

I Can Cook!

CHINESE FOOD

Wendy
Blaxland

A⁺

Smart Apple Media
P.O. Box 3263
Mankato, MN, 56002

Reprinted 2012

First published in 2011 by
MACMILLAN EDUCATION AUSTRALIA PTY LTD
15–19 Claremont St, South Yarra, Australia 3141

Visit our website at www.macmillan.com.au or go directly to www.macmillanlibrary.com.au

Associated companies and representatives throughout the world.

Copyright text © Wendy Blaxland 2011

Library of Congress Cataloging-in-Publication Data

Blaxland, Wendy.
    Chinese food / Wendy Blaxland.
        p. cm. — (I can cook!)
    Summary:"Describes historical, cultural, and geographical factors that have influenced the cuisine of China. Includes
    recipes to create Chinese food"— Provided by publisher.
    Includes index.
    ISBN 978-1-59920-671-4 (library binding)
    1. Cooking, Chinese—Juvenile literature. 2. Cookbooks. I. Title.
    TX724.5.C5B53 2012
641.5951—dc22
                                2011005448

Publisher: Carmel Heron
Commissioning Editor: Niki Horin
Managing Editor: Vanessa Lanaway
Editor: Laura Jeanne Gobal
Proofreaders: Georgina Garner; Kirstie Innes–Will
Designer: Stella Vassiliou
Page Layout: Stella Vassiliou
Photo Researcher: Claire Armstrong (management: Debbie Gallagher)
Illustrators: Jacki Sosenko; Guy Holt (map, **7**, **9**); Gregory Baldwin (map icons, **9**)
Production Controller: Vanessa Johnson

Manufactured in China by Macmillan Production (Asia) Ltd.
Kwun Tong, Kowloon, Hong Kong
Supplier Code: CP March 2011

Acknowledgments

The author would like to thank the following for their generous help and expert advice: Emeritus Professor Eugene Anderson, University of California; Lynne Olver, editor, FoodTimeline; and Dena Saulsbury-Monaco, librarian and cook, Montreal.

The author and the publisher are grateful to the following for permission to reproduce copyright material:

Front cover photographs: Chinese dumplings courtesy of Dreamstime/Smokefish; vegetable spring rolls courtesy of iStockphoto.com/8by5; sweet orange tea courtesy of MEA Photos; cashew chicken courtesy of Shutterstock/Mark Stout Photography; egg flower soup courtesy of Shutterstock/mikeledray.
Back cover photographs: Brown paper bag courtesy of Shutterstock/Nils Z; tomato egg flower soup courtesy of Christine Wong; chilies courtesy of Shutterstock/Jiang Hongyan; capsicums courtesy of Shutterstock/Hal_P; Chinese cabbage courtesy of Shutterstock/Elena Schweitzer; and raddish leaves courtesy of Shutterstock/sunsetman.

Photographs courtesy of: AAP/AP Photo/Vincent Thian, **28** (left); Corbis/Steven Vidler, **6** (dumplings); Getty Images/Alexandra Panella, **15** (top left); iStockphoto.com/ajafoto, **10** (tea towel), /Alina555, **14**, **15** (star anise), /Antagain, **26** (banana), **27** (sliced banana), /bedo, **30** (center), /brinkstock, **13** (clipboard), /Paul Cowan, **6** (rice & chopsticks), /dkgilbey, **14** (cinnamon sticks), **15** (cinnamon sticks), /gbh007, **4** (boy), /hippostudio, **6** (steam basket), **8** (steam basket), /Jamesmcq24, **19** (green onions), **21** (green onions), /KingWu, **30** (bottom), /luxcreative, **27** (top right), /Robyn Mac, **10** (hanging utensils), /mstroz, **23** (snow peas), /Urosh Petrovic, **throughout** (red oven mitt), /Viktar, **24** (bottom left), **25** (top right); MEA Photos, **25** (top left); Photolibrary/Alamy/© Peter Tsai Photography, **28** (right), /Artemi Kyriacou, **23** (chicken stir-fry), /Lawrence Migdale, **29**, /TAO Images Limited, **21** (top left); Shutterstock/Aaron Amat, **11** (grater), /Anat-oli, **9** (pig), /Mark Aplet, **13** (electric mixer), /artproem, **8** (fish), /bgfreestyler, **27** (limes), /bonchan, **7** (bottom left), /Adrian Britton, **10** (baking tray), /Darren Brode, **11** (electric mixer), /buriy, **8** (rice), **9** (rice), /Ilker Canikligil, **10** (saucepan), **13** (saucepan), /ZH Chen, **10** (measuring cups), /Colour, **8** (chicken), /Coprid, **13** (soap dispenser), /Luis Francisco Cordero, **10** (whisk), /Mikael Damkier, **10** (frying pan, measuring jug), /Raphael Daniaud, **11** (blender), /discpicture, **6** (tea), /ejwhite, **11** (colander), /Christopher Elwell, **8** (watermelon), /eskay, **10** (wok), /FCG, **9** (sheep), /Iakov Filimonov, **13** (knives), /Gregory Gerber, **8** (crabs), /Gilmanshin, **13** (knife block), **31**, /Goncharuk, **9** (corn), /grublee, **18** (tomatoes), **19** (tomatoes), /Chris Green, **7** (top right), /Shawn Hempel, **27** (bottom left), /Jiang Hongyan, **8** (chilies, prawns, winter melon), **9** (prawns, winter melon), /Danylchenko Iaroslav, **17** (spring rolls), /infografick, **8** (eggs), /Tischenko Irina, **10** (butter knife, large knife), /Eric Isselée, **9** (horses, yak), /K13 ART, **8** (green bowl), **11** (bowls), /Kayros Studio, **13** (fire extinguisher), /Keattikorn, **8** (bamboo shoots), /Tamara Kulikova, **8** (noodles), /Wolfe Larry, **22** (chilies), /LazarevDN, **10** (sieve), /Chris Leachman, **10** (chopping board), /Eric Lee/Photos Art, **7** (top left), /Hao Liang, **8** (mushrooms), /LittleMiss, **9** (Chinese pears), /Madlen, **9** (lychees), /Petr Malyshev, **13** (kettle), /Marco Mayer, **8** (barley), /Iain McGillivray, **10** (tongs), /MdN, **8** (Chinese plums), /Melica, **4** (vegetables), **5** (vegetables), **17** (vegetables), /mimo, **24** (pair oranges), **25** (pair oranges), /Monkey Business Images, **5** (girl), /Mopic, **13** (first-aid box), /Lisovskaya Natalia, **23** (carrots), /Nattika, **8** (eggplant), /Kristina Postnikova, **4** (chopsticks), **10** (chopsticks), **21** (chopsticks), /Ragnarock, **11** (slotted spoon), **13** (frying pan), /Stephen Aaron Rees, **11** (wooden spoon), /Jess Reika, **8** (water spinach), /Anatoliy Samara, **9** (wheat), /Elena Schweitzer, **8** (Chinese cabbage), **9** (Chinese cabbage) /Roman Sika, **8** (garlic), /soncerina, **10** (fork), /Soyka, **9** (buckwheat), /stanislaff, **8** (pork), /STILLFX, **10** (peeler), /sunsetman, **8** (white raddish), /Ev Thomas, **13** (fire blanket), /Andrey Tiyk, **9** (pineapple), /Kheng Guan Toh, **7** (bottom right), /Matt Valentine, **10** (bread knife), /GraÃ§a Victoria, **10** (oven mitts), **13** (oven mitts), /Vlue, **10** (steak knife), /Valentyn Volkov, **8** (carrots), /Xebeche, **8** (oranges), /Pan Xunbin, **9** (crab), /zkruger, **30** (top), /zcw, **8** (Chinese jujubes); Christine Wong, **19** (top left).

While every care has been taken to trace and acknowledge copyright, the publisher tenders their apologies for any accidental infringement where copyright has proved untraceable. They would be pleased to come to a suitable arrangement with the rightful owner in each case.

Contents

Glossary Words

When a word is printed in **bold**, it is explained in the Glossary on page 31.

Cooking tips

Safety Warning

Ask an adult for help when you see this red oven mitt on a recipe.

How To

Cooking techniques are explained in small boxes with this handprint.

Some of the events in this book happened a long time ago, more than 2,000 years ago. To understand this, people measure time in years Before the Common Era (BCE) and during the Common Era (CE). It looks like this on a timeline.

| Years BCE | 150 | 100 | 50 | 0 | 50 | 100 | 150 | Years CE |

I Can Cook!

Cooking is a rewarding and lifelong skill. With some basic cooking knowledge, a little practice, and great recipes, you can cook entire meals! Cooking for your family and friends is a fun activity, and a mouthwatering meal can take you to places that you have never been. Are you ready to have fun cooking—and eating?

A World of Food

Every day, people all over the world cook delicious and **nutritious** meals. What they cook depends not only on the ingredients available to them, but also on their country's food **culture** or cooking style. A country's style of cooking is shaped over time by its culture, **economy**, **climate** and the land itself.

Cook Your Way Around the World

You can explore the great cuisines of the world in your own kitchen. The special flavors and wonderful aromas of a country's food culture come from fresh ingredients and particular spices or herbs, which you can find in your local supermarket or a specialty store. Share with your family and friends authentic dishes from different countries that look great and taste even better.

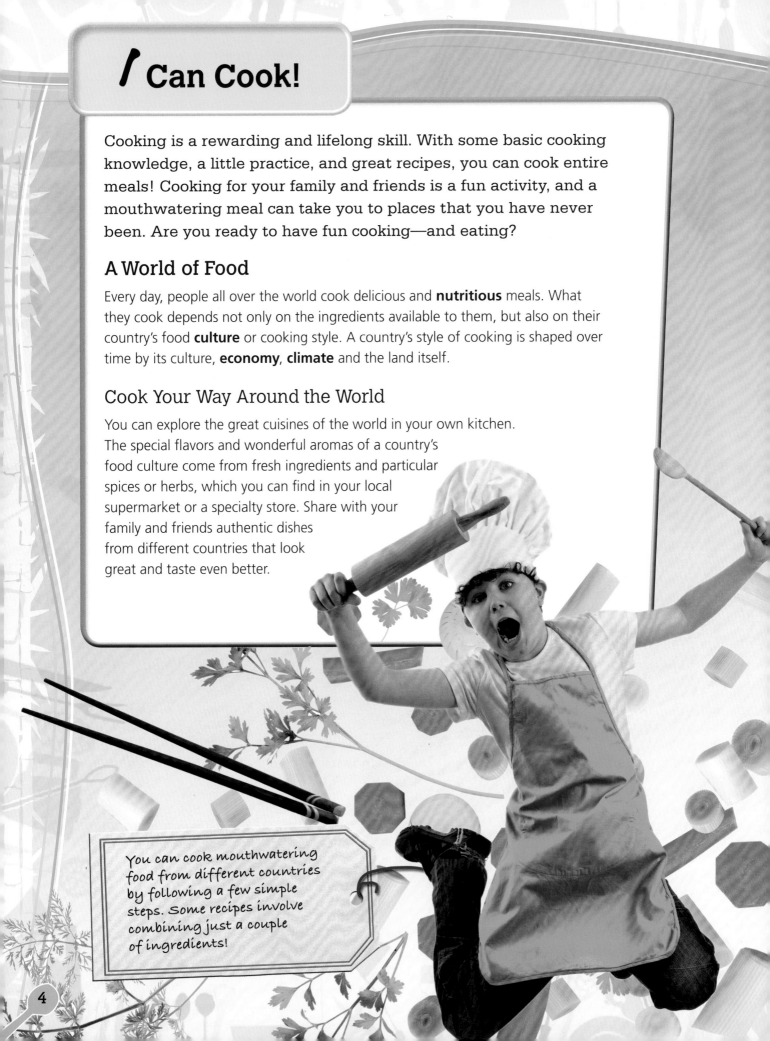

You can cook mouthwatering food from different countries by following a few simple steps. Some recipes involve combining just a couple of ingredients!

Chinese Food

Chinese Food Worldwide

Chinese food has been taken by the Chinese all over the world, changing to suit its new surroundings and the ingredients available. This has led to the creation of new Chinese dishes, such as chow mein in the United States (U.S.) and Manchurian chicken in India.

The Chinese enjoy eating together. Chinese food aims to balance colors, textures, and tastes, as recommended by the ancient Chinese thinker Confucius, and to keep people healthy, as Taoism, a Chinese religion and way of thinking, suggests.

The Principles of Chinese Cooking

Confucius taught that food should delight the senses and balance the elements, such as hot and cold. His teachings are followed, for example, in the combination of colors usually found in a quick stir-fry, the elegant presentation of Cantonese dishes to please the eye, and the way Szechuan cooking balances the tastes of fiery chilies and peppers with sweet beet sugar, sour pickled vegetables, and flavored salts. Confucius also believed in good table manners and rules for the preparation of food, such as cutting food into bite-sized pieces before cooking so knives are not needed at the table.

Cooking Chinese Food at Home

It is surprisingly easy to create a colorful and satisfying Chinese meal at home. If you can boil water, you can make tea eggs for a snack! This book has seven recipes that you can follow to cook a meal on your own or with a little help from an adult. Some of the recipes don't even involve cooking. The recipes can be adapted to suit special **diets**, too.

China is known officially as the People's Republic of China. It is located in Asia.

Chinese food can be a simple dish of rice topped with meat and vegetables, eaten with a pair of chopsticks!

Traditions and Styles

China is a huge country with a wide range of peoples, landscapes, climates, and cultural **traditions**. As a result, Chinese cooking styles offer a staggering variety of recipes. However, they are all still instantly recognized as Chinese cooking.

These are some of the essentials of Chinese food (from top right): rice and tea, which are **native** to China, and dumplings, which can be enjoyed in many ways.

The Importance of Grains

The **fertile** rice-growing river basins of China have been home to the Chinese **civilization** since 4000 BCE. Rice has often been the only food available to the poor of China's ever-increasing population. A bowl of rice is usually topped with a few vegetables, such as shallots, bean sprouts, and Chinese cabbage, flavored with ginger or garlic. Small pieces of meat, including chicken or pork, are added when available.

However, rice cannot be grown in the north because the climate is too cold. Here, millet and sorghum, two kinds of grains, have become **staple foods**. These are often eaten as porridge. Here, too, wheat is generally made into dumplings and noodles.

Regional Food

Chinese food is united by its balance of sweet, salty, sour, and hot tastes. However, styles of cooking and important flavors vary from region to region. The map below breaks China up into four main regions and discusses the ingredients and special foods that are popular in each.

Chinese Vegetarian Food

There are many delicious vegetarian Chinese recipes. This is because in the early days, many people could not afford to buy meat. It is also due to the strong **Buddhist** tradition in China. Buddhists believe that animals should not be harmed.

North

Northern cooking is based on dishes made from wheat flour, such as dumplings, stuffed buns, steamed bread, and noodles. One famous dish is Peking duck (pictured), which is roast duck wrapped in small, thin pancakes, served with hoisin sauce.

MONGOLIA

NORTH KOREA

SOUTH KOREA

NORTH

Yellow Sea

EAST

WEST

NEPAL

BHUTAN

INDIA

BANGLADESH

MYANMAR

VIETNAM

LAOS

SOUTH

TAIWAN

East

Eastern Chinese cooking prides itself on fresh ingredients, especially seafood, and light, sweet flavors. Famous dishes include egg cakes (pictured).

THAILAND

Bay of Bengal

South China Sea

CAMBODIA

West

Szechuan food from Sichuan Province is well known for its spicy heat. This province grows some of the world's hottest chillies. The famous dish *mapo tofu* (pictured) uses spicy tofu and minced meat. Cooking techniques include stir-frying and dry-roasting. Food is also preserved through salting, drying, and smoking.

South

Cantonese cooking from Guangdong Province uses light flavors and techniques, such as steaming and stir-frying, which preserve the freshness of the ingredients. Cantonese cooks also present their food beautifully. Dim sum (pictured) is a Cantonese specialty that offers small portions of a huge variety of food.

Chinese Ingredients

Most Chinese eat rice topped with vegetables and meat. However, north of the Yellow River, noodles, dumplings, and bread are eaten more often than rice. These are cooked with a wide variety of vegetables, eggs, meat, and seafood, and flavored with a range of sauces made from soybean paste, garlic, or chilies.

Meat
Chinese cooking uses pork and chicken as well as meat from more unusual sources, such as frogs and even insects. Beef is less common.

Seafood
Fish and other seafood, such as shrimp and crabs, are popular along the coast and near rivers. Less common Chinese seafood includes abalone and sea cucumber.

Fruit
Fruit is not widely used in Chinese cooking. However, oranges are enjoyed for dessert, as well as peaches and melons in the north. Less well-known fruits include *mei*, a type of apricot, and jujubes, or Chinese dates. Watermelons are popular for their flesh and seeds.

Staple Foods
Rice is the main staple food. However, in the colder north, noodles and dumplings are the staples. These are usually made from wheat flour. Other northern staple grains include corn, barley, and millet.

Dairy Products
The Chinese make little use of dairy products, such as cheese and yogurt.

Vegetables
In the north, the main vegetable is Chinese cabbage. Other common vegetables include spinach, carrots, white radishes, bamboo shoots, eggplant, mushrooms, chilies, and winter melons.

Landscapes and Climates

China has a mountainous south, two major river valleys, and high, grassy, inland plains. It also has a very long eastern coast. These different landscapes create different climates that allow a wide range of food to be grown. The map below shows which areas of the country China's produce comes from.

Wheat is grown mainly in northern, central, and western China.

Kumis, or fermented mare's milk, is an important drink to the Mongols of the high central Chinese plateau.

Onions, garlic, and cabbage are grown in the cold north.

Corn, soybeans, and millet are grown in the cold north.

KAZAKHSTAN

MONGOLIA

Pigs, ducks, and chickens are raised in central China.

NORTH

Sheep are farmed in the central north.

Yellow Sea

Yaks are raised on the Tibetan plateau.

WEST

EAST

NEPAL

BHUTAN

INDIA

BANGLADESH

SOUTH

China's eastern coastal waters and its rivers and **deltas** provide large and small fish, such as bream and carp, and a range of seafood, including shrimp, crabs, and squid.

Barley and buckwheat are grown in cold mountainous areas, such as the Tibetan plateau.

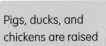

MYANMAR

VIETNAM

LAOS

Bay of Bengal

THAILAND

South China Sea

Tropical fruits, such as lychees and pineapples, are grown in the south. Chilies are grown in Sichuan Province.

Rice is grown in central and southeastern China, where two crops are harvested a year.

Many root and leafy vegetables are grown in the fertile valleys of the Yellow and Yangtze rivers, along with eggplant, gourds, such as winter melon, and fruits, including apricots, apples, and pears.

Cooking Basics

Equipment

Having the right equipment to cook with is very important. Here are some of the most common items needed in the kitchen.

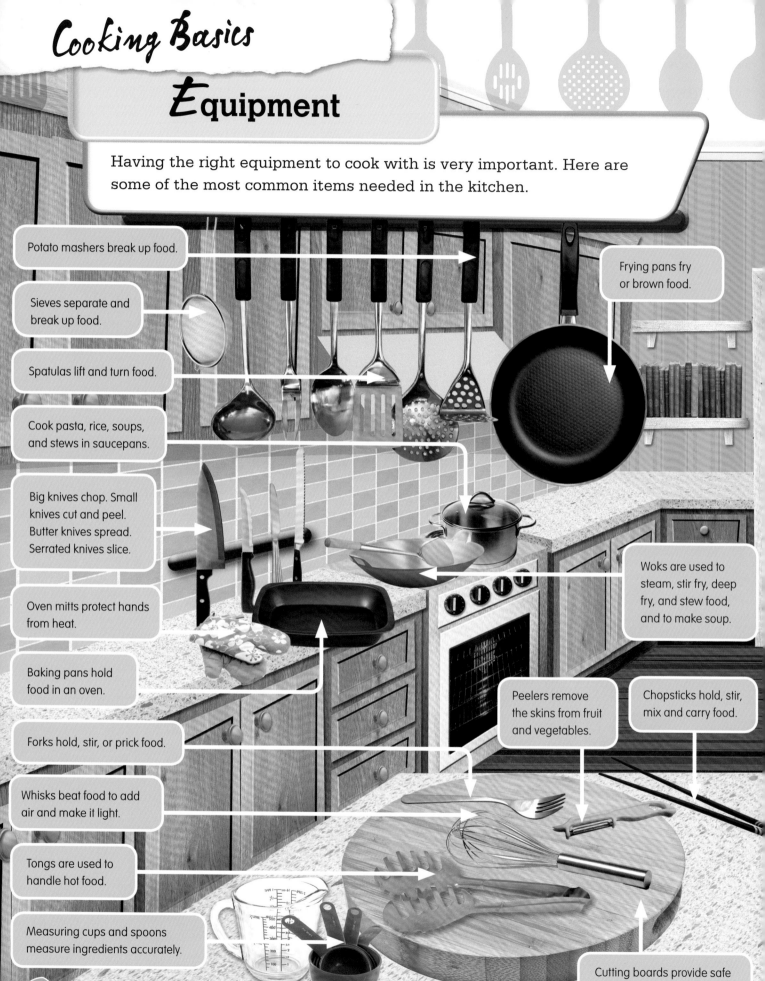

Potato mashers break up food.

Sieves separate and break up food.

Spatulas lift and turn food.

Cook pasta, rice, soups, and stews in saucepans.

Big knives chop. Small knives cut and peel. Butter knives spread. Serrated knives slice.

Oven mitts protect hands from heat.

Baking pans hold food in an oven.

Forks hold, stir, or prick food.

Whisks beat food to add air and make it light.

Tongs are used to handle hot food.

Measuring cups and spoons measure ingredients accurately.

Frying pans fry or brown food.

Woks are used to steam, stir fry, deep fry, and stew food, and to make soup.

Peelers remove the skins from fruit and vegetables.

Chopsticks hold, stir, mix and carry food.

Cutting boards provide safe surfaces for cutting food.

Blenders chop ingredients, mix food, and make smooth sauces and soups.

Spoons mix and stir. Wooden spoons prevent scratched pans. Slotted spoons let liquid drain away.

Graters shave thin slices from food, such as cheese.

Colanders drain liquids.

Mixers mix food quickly.

Bowls hold food for mixing.

11

Cooking Basics

Weight, Volume, Temperature, and Special Diets

It is important to use the right amount of ingredients, cook at the correct heat, and be aware of people with special dietary needs.

Weight and Volume

The weight and volume of ingredients can be measured with a weighing scale or with measuring cups and spoons. Convert them using this table. Measure dry ingredients so that they are level across the top of the spoon or cup without packing them down.

Recipe Measurement	Weight	Volume
1 cup	8 ounces	250 ml
½ cup	4 ounces	125 ml
2 tablespoons	1 ounce	30 ml
1 teaspoon	0.16 ounce	4.7 ml

Temperature

Fahrenheit and Celsius are two different ways of measuring temperature. Oven dials may show the temperature in either Fahrenheit or Celsius. Use lower temperatures in gas or convection ovens.

Oven Temperature	Celsius	Fahrenheit
Slow	150°	300°
Moderately slow	160°–170°	320°–340°
Moderate	180°	350°
Moderately hot	190°	375°
Hot	200°	400°
Very hot	220°–240°	430°–470°

Special Diets

Some people follow special diets because of personal or religious beliefs about what they should eat. Others must not eat certain foods because they are **allergic** to them.

Diet	What It Means	Symbol
Allergy-specific	Some people's bodies react to a certain food as if it were poison. They may die from eating even a tiny amount of this food. Nuts, eggs, milk, strawberries, and even chocolate may cause allergic reactions.	
Halal	**Muslims** eat only food prepared according to strict religious guidelines. This is called halal food.	
Kosher	**Jews** eat only food prepared according to strict religious guidelines. This is called kosher food.	
Vegan	Vegans eat nothing from animals, including dairy products, eggs, and honey.	
Vegetarian	Vegetarians eat no animal products and may or may not eat dairy products, eggs, and honey.	

Safety and Hygiene

Be safe in the kitchen by staying alert and using equipment correctly when cooking. Practicing good food hygiene means you always serve clean, germ-free food. Follow the handy tips below!

Be Organized

Hungry? Organized cooks eat sooner! First, read the recipe. Next, take out the equipment and ingredients you'll need and follow the stages set out in the recipe. Straighten up and clean as you go. While your food cooks, wash up, sweep the kitchen floor, and empty the garbage.

Heat

Place boiling saucepans toward the back of the stove with handles turned inward. Keep your hands and face away from steam and switch hot equipment off as soon as you have finished using it. Use oven mitts to pick up hot pots and put them down on heatproof surfaces. Always check that food is cool enough to eat.

Emergencies

All kitchens should have a fire blanket, fire extinguisher, and first-aid box.

Food Hygiene

To avoid spreading germs, wash your hands well and keep coughs and sneezes away from food. Use fresh ingredients and always store food that spoils easily, such as meat and fish, in the refrigerator.

Electricity

Use electrical equipment only with an adult's help. Switch the power off before unplugging any equipment, and keep it away from water.

Knives

When cutting food with a knife, cut away from yourself and onto a nonslip surface, such as a suitable cutting board.

13

Tea Eggs

Tea eggs are also called "golden treasures," They are often given to family and friends during the Chinese New Year as symbols of good fortune. Tea eggs are flavored by simmering them in spiced tea. Each egg, with its delicate spiderweb of patterns, is unique. These patterns are made by gently cracking the eggshells.

MAKES: 6 tea eggs

PREPARATION TIME: 5 minutes

COOKING TIME: 2½ hours

FOOD VALUES: About 70 **calories**, 5 grams of fat, 6 grams of **protein**, and 1 gram of **carbohydrates** per egg.

SPECIAL DIETS: Suitable for vegetarian, nut-free, dairy-free and **gluten**-free diets. For kosher and halal diets, use certified ingredients; for vegan diets, try making "eggs" with firm cubes of tofu coated with a thin flour paste and dried.

Equipment

- Tablespoon
- Medium-size saucepan with lid
- Slotted spoon
- Tea towel
- Medium-size bowl

Ingredients

- 6 eggs
- 8 cups of water
- 3 tablespoons of Lapsang Souchong tea leaves (ordinary tea and tea bags will do, too)
- ½ cup of low-salt dark soy sauce
- 1 cinnamon stick (optional)
- 1 whole star anise (optional)

What to Do

1

Place the eggs in the saucepan and cover them with water. Bring the water to the boil, then simmer for 10–12 minutes.

2

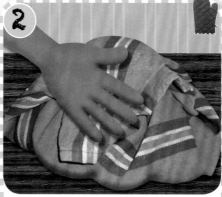

Lift the eggs out of the saucepan with a slotted spoon and place them on the tea towel. When the eggs have cooled, gently crack the shells all over by rolling them in the tea towel while applying gentle pressure or by using the back of a spoon to tap the eggs. Note: Keep the shells on the eggs—the shells should be just cracked.

3

Empty the saucepan and fill it again with the 8 cups of water. Put the tea leaves, soy sauce, cinnamon, and 2 points of the star anise (if using the spices) in the saucepan.

Recipe Variations

Try three different food colorings instead of using tea.

Experiment with tapping the eggs sharply at different points for a starburst effect.

Ask an adult for help with using the stove.

4

Add the eggs to the saucepan and bring the water slowly to a boil. Next, turn the heat down, cover the saucepan, and simmer for 1 hour.

5

With help from an adult, remove the saucepan from the stove. Let the eggs and liquid cool. When the eggs are cool, remove them from the saucepan. Store them in the bowl in the refrigerator until needed.

6

Just before serving, remove the shells. Every egg will have a different pattern!

Spring Rolls

Long ago in China, spring rolls were eaten on the first day of spring to ward off evil. These early spring rolls used the first fresh vegetables of the season. Now, meat, seafood, or vegetables may be mixed and wrapped in thin dough, then deep-fried, steamed, or eaten raw. Spring rolls are popular snacks all over Southeast Asia, too.

MAKES: 3 spring rolls

PREPARATION TIME: 30 minutes

COOKING TIME: 10 minutes

FOOD VALUES: About 90 calories, 5 g of fat, 6 g of protein, and 11 g of carbohydrates per spring roll, depending on the filling.

SPECIAL DIETS: Suitable for vegan, vegetarian, nut-free, and halal diets, depending on the filling. For gluten-free diets, use gluten-free rice paper wrappers; and for kosher diets, use certified wrappers.

Equipment
- Wooden spoon
- Small saucepan
- Serving bowl
- Frying pan (or wok)
- Shallow dish (large enough for spring roll wrappers to lie flat)
- Serving plate

Ingredients
- 1 teaspoon of canola oil
- 2 cups of mixed vegetables (try cabbage, carrot, celery, and water chestnuts), chopped evenly
- 3 spring roll wrappers plus spares

FOR DIPPING SAUCE
- 2 cloves of garlic, finely chopped
- ¼ cup of soy sauce
- ¼ cup of water
- 1 teaspoon of corn flour
- 2 tablespoons of rice vinegar
- 2 tablespoons of sugar

What to Do

Place the garlic in the saucepan with the other ingredients for the dipping sauce. Heat the mixture on the stove over low heat for 3–5 minutes until the sugar dissolves and the corn flour is mixed in. Pour the dipping sauce into the serving bowl and set it aside to cool.

Pour the oil into the frying pan and heat it on the stove at high heat. Add the chopped vegetables and lightly *sauté* them. Let the vegetables cool.

Fill the shallow dish halfway with warm water. Soak 3 spring roll wrappers in the dish for about 20 seconds or until they are flexible.

Heat the oil on high heat, then add the chopped vegetables. Move the vegetables about frequently so that each piece cooks evenly. Cook the vegetables for about 4 minutes.

Recipe Variations

With help from an adult, fry the spring rolls in ½-inch-deep oil, turning them gently once, for crispy, hot spring rolls.

Try other dipping sauces, such as sweet chili, peanut, or sweet and sour sauce.

Ask an adult for help with using the stove.

4 Take one wrapper out and place it on a flat surface. If the wrapper tears, use two. Put ⅓ of the vegetables in a line across the middle of the wrapper, leaving about ½ inch at either end so the wrapper can be folded.

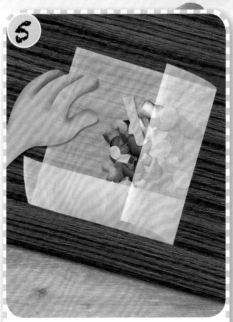

5 Prepare the spring roll by folding the bottom flap of the wrapper over the vegetables. Do the same with the sides, then the top, to make a neat package.

6 Repeat steps 4 and 5 until all of the spring rolls are ready. Arrange them on the serving plate and serve with the dipping sauce.

Let's Cook!

Tomato Egg Flower Soup

The name of this soup, also known as "egg drop soup," celebrates the way the eggs form petal-like threads as they are gently stirred into the soup. Tomatoes were added to this dish in the 1900s CE. Cooks in different Chinese regions may add extra ingredients, such as tofu or bean sprouts.

Equipment

- 2 medium-size saucepans
- Wooden spoon
- Colander
- Grater
- Small, sharp knife
- Cutting board
- Small bowl
- Fork (or whisk)
- Tablespoon

Ingredients

- 2 cups of roughly chopped vegetables, including skins and stalks (try carrots, celery, and onions)
- 4 cups of water
- ½ inch of ginger
- 2 scallions
- 1 can of chopped tomatoes (14 oz)
- 1 tablespoon of soy sauce
- 2 eggs

What to Do

1 Add the vegetables to water in a saucepan and bring to a boil. Simmer for about 40 minutes. Carefully strain the stock into the other saucepan and throw away the vegetables.

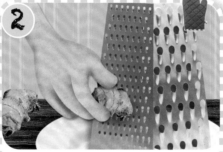

2 Grate enough ginger to fill a teaspoon. Next, peel the scallions and chop them finely. Set the scallions aside.

3 Add the can of chopped tomatoes, ginger, and scallions to the stock. Stir well and bring the soup to a boil.

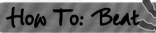

How To: Beat

Mix the eggs very quickly with the fork.

Recipe Variations

For a heartier soup, add noodles before making the egg flowers.
Garnish the soup with chopped parsley or cilantro.

Ask an adult for help with using the knife and stove.

4

Add the soy sauce, then reduce the heat and allow the soup to simmer or boil slowly.

5

Crack the eggs into the bowl and **beat** them with the fork until they are well mixed.

6

Create the egg "flowers" by drizzling the egg mixture slowly into the soup while stirring quickly with a fork to form silky threads. Continue to stir in one direction for at least a minute. Let the soup sit for 3 minutes before serving.

Chinese Dumplings

Dumplings are enjoyed at all celebrations, but especially during Chinese New Year. They are shaped like ancient Chinese gold bars and are symbols of wealth. On the eve of Chinese New Year, the whole family gathers to make and eat dumplings. One dumpling may contain a hidden coin for extra luck!

MAKES: about 30 dumplings

PREPARATION TIME: 30 minutes

COOKING TIME: 5–10 minutes

FOOD VALUES: About 100 calories and 6 g of carbohydrates per dumpling. No fat or protein.

SPECIAL DIETS: Suitable for nut-free diets. For vegan and vegetarian diets, exclude meat and use only vegetables, tofu, and herbs; for gluten-free diets, use rice flour instead of wheat flour; and for kosher and halal diets, use certified meat.

Equipment

- 2 bowls
- Wooden spoon
- Clean, damp tea towel
- Teaspoon
- Rolling pin
- Tablespoon
- Large saucepan
- Slotted spoon

Ingredients

FOR WRAPPERS

- A pinch of salt
- 1½ cups of plain flour
- About ¾ cup of cold water

FOR FILLING

- ½ cup of ground pork or beef
- 2 teaspoons of soy sauce
- 4 teaspoons of sesame oil
- ¼ scallion, finely chopped
- ¾ cup of finely shredded Chinese cabbage
- 2 tablespoons of shredded bamboo shoots (canned will do)
- ¼ inch of fresh ginger, finely chopped
- ½ clove of garlic, finely chopped
- A pinch of freshly ground white pepper (optional)

What to Do

1 To make the wrappers, first mix the salt with the flour. Next, slowly stir in the cold water, a quarter of a cup at a time, adding just enough to form a smooth dough.

2 Dust your hands and the work surface with a little spare flour. **Knead** the dough into a smooth, elastic ball. Cover it with the damp tea towel and let it rest for at least 30 minutes.

3 While the dough is resting, prepare the filling. Mix the meat well with the soy sauce, sesame oil, scallion, cabbage, bamboo shoots, ginger, garlic, and pepper. Set aside.

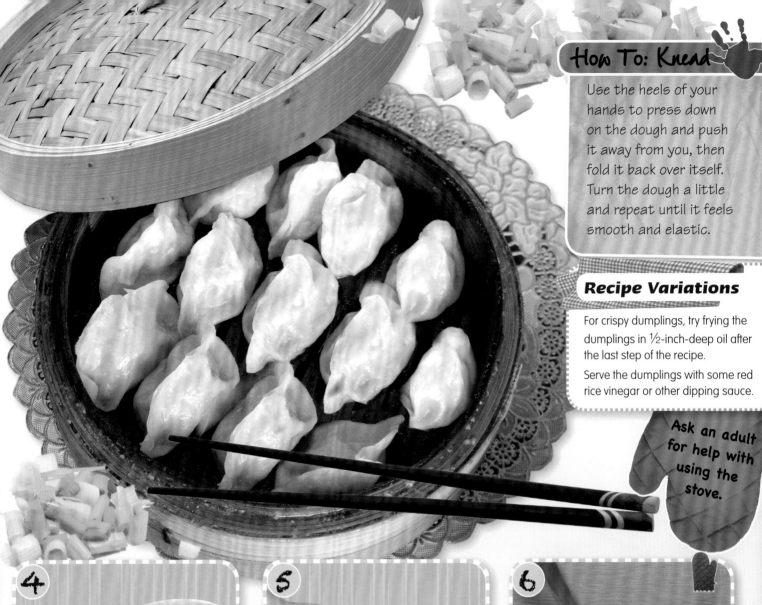

How To: Knead

Use the heels of your hands to press down on the dough and push it away from you, then fold it back over itself. Turn the dough a little and repeat until it feels smooth and elastic.

Recipe Variations

For crispy dumplings, try frying the dumplings in ½-inch-deep oil after the last step of the recipe.

Serve the dumplings with some red rice vinegar or other dipping sauce.

Ask an adult for help with using the stove.

4

Knead the dough again until it forms a smooth ball. Then divide it into 30 small balls. Using the rolling pin, roll each ball into a circle with a diameter of about 3 inches. Sprinkle a little extra flour on the rolling pin if the dough begins to stick.

5

Place about 1 level tablespoon of the filling in the middle of a wrapper. Wet the edge of the wrapper with water. Fold the flaps of the wrapper over to form a half-moon shape, and pinch the edge to seal it. Repeat this with all of the dumplings.

6

Bring a large saucepan of water to a boil. Add half of the dumplings to the water, stirring them gently to stop them from sticking together. Cook them for 5–10 minutes until the dough is soft. Remove the dumplings with the slotted spoon. Repeat this step with the remaining dumplings.

Chicken and Cashew Stir-fry

This Cantonese dish uses the technique of stir-frying, which became popular during the Han Dynasty (206 BCE–200 CE). Fuel was scarce, and people needed a way to cook quickly, using little oil. Cutting the ingredients into small pieces and cooking them fast in a very hot pan seals in the flavors and colors.

SERVES: 3

PREPARATION TIME: 20 minutes

COOKING TIME: 12 minutes

FOOD VALUES: About 222 calories, 9 g of fat, 6 g of protein, and 29 g of carbohydrates per serving.

SPECIAL DIETS: Suitable for gluten-free diets. For vegan and vegetarian diets, use tofu instead of chicken and use vegetable bouillon; for nut-free diets, use toasted sunflower or pumpkin seeds instead of cashew nuts; and for kosher and halal diets, use certified meat.

Equipment

- Small, sharp knife
- Cutting board
- 3 bowls
- Wok (or frying pan)
- Wooden spoon
- Fork

Ingredients

- ½ pound of chicken breast fillet
- 2 teaspoons of canola oil
- ½ teaspoon of sesame oil
- ½ clove of garlic, sliced
- ¼ inch of ginger, grated
- 1 shallot, finely sliced
- ½ of a chili, finely sliced
- ½ of a carrot, sliced
- ¼ pound snow peas, trimmed
- ¾ cup of chicken stock
- ½ tablespoon of corn flour mixed with 2 tablespoons of water
- ½ tablespoon of sesame seeds
- 1 tablespoon of cilantro, chopped
- ½ cup of cashew nuts, toasted
- 2 cups of cooked rice

What to Do

1 Cut the chicken fillet into cubes that are about ¼ inch thick.

2 Heat the wok until it is very hot. Add most of the canola and sesame oils and swirl them around. Add the chicken in batches and cook until it is just browned (about 3 minutes). Keep the food moving so that it cooks quickly. Next, remove the chicken from the wok and set aside.

3 Add the garlic, ginger, shallots, and chili to the wok and fry until fragrant.

Recipe Variations

Serve with noodles instead of rice. Just soak some noodles in hot water and heat them quickly in the wok with a little sesame oil once the chicken and vegetables are ready.

Choose your favorite vegetables. Look for brightly colored vegetables, such as yellow, green, or red bell peppers, purple eggplant, or green beans.

Ask an adult for help with using the knife and stove. You might also like to wear gloves when slicing the chili.

4

Add a little more oil to the wok, then add the carrots and snow peas. Cook until the vegetables are just tender (about 2–3 minutes). Set aside. Using the fork, remove the chili slices and throw them away.

5

Add the stock, corn flour mixture, and sesame seeds to the wok. Bring to a boil. Reduce the heat and cook until the sauce starts to thicken.

6

Return the vegetables, chicken, and flavorings to the wok. Sprinkle the cilantro and cashews over them. Serve immediately with steamed rice.

Let's Cook!

MAKES: 4 glasses

PREPARATION TIME: 7 minutes

COOKING TIME: 10 minutes

FOOD VALUES: About 80 calories and 21 g of carbohydrates per glass. No fat or protein.

SPECIAL DIETS: Suitable for vegan, vegetarian, nut-free, gluten-free, kosher, and halal diets.

Sweet Orange Tea

Like all citrus fruit, oranges are considered lucky in China. Tangerines, a type of orange, are presented to family and friends during Chinese New Year to wish them good fortune. Sweet orange tea is served at Chinese banquets to refresh the tastebuds between courses.

Equipment

- Cutting board
- Small, sharp knife
- Citrus juicer
- Medium-size bowl
- Large saucepan
- Wooden spoon
- 4 tall glasses

Ingredients

- 6 medium-size oranges
- 3 cups of water
- 1/3 cup of brown sugar
- 1/3 cup of white sugar
- 1 tablespoon of corn flour

Recipe Variations

Add a few drops of orange blossom water and orange zest to the mixture before serving to strengthen the flavor.

Create a festive look by wetting the rims of the glasses and dipping them in powdered sugar before carefully filling each glass. Garnish with slices of orange.

What to Do

1 Roll each orange on the cutting board to free the juice inside. Next, cut each orange in half.

2 Use the citrus juicer to squeeze the juice out of the oranges. Pour the juice and pulp into the bowl.

Ask an adult for help with using the knife and stove.

3

Pour the water into the saucepan. Add the two types of sugar and the corn flour to the water, and bring the mixture to a boil, stirring constantly.

4

Pour the orange juice and pulp into the saucepan and stir.

5

To enjoy this drink while hot, pour the sweet orange tea into four glasses and serve. Otherwise, allow to cool before pouring into a pitcher and refrigerating.

MAKES: 4 glazed bananas

PREPARATION TIME: 10 minutes

COOKING TIME: 10 minutes

FOOD VALUES: About 431 calories, 15 g of fat, 19 g of protein, and 59 g of carbohydrates per banana.

SPECIAL DIETS: Suitable for vegan, vegetarian, gluten-free, nut-free, kosher, and halal diets.

Recipe Variations

Dust the banana slices with sugar and a pinch of cinnamon or nutmeg powder for a spicy flavor.

If nut allergies are not a problem, sprinkle some chopped pecans, peanuts, or other favorite nuts over the bananas.

Glazed Bananas

Bananas have been grown on plantations in southern China since 200 CE, though they have been widely eaten only since transportation improved during the 1900s CE. The Chinese have also made cane sugar in the south since ancient times. Glazed bananas is a delicious dessert with a crunchy toffee covering that is popular in Chinese restaurants.

Equipment

- Grater (or zester)
- Small plate
- Cutting board
- Small, sharp knife
- Citrus juicer
- Measuring spoons
- Serving plate
- Small saucepan
- Wooden spoon

Ingredients

- 2 limes (optional)
- 4 medium-size ripe but firm bananas
- ½ cup of brown sugar
- 4 tablespoons of butter (or margarine), melted
- 1/3 cup of sesame seeds

What to Do

1 If using, grate the skin of the limes to make about 2 teaspoons of lime zest. Do not use the bitter, white pith.

2 Roll each lime on the cutting board to free the juice inside. Cut each lime in half and use the citrus juicer to make 2 tablespoons of lime juice.

Ask an adult for help with using the knife and stove.

Peel the bananas and cut them diagonally into slices that are ½ inch wide. Pile the slices on the serving plate.

Combine the sugar and butter in the saucepan and stir it over medium heat until it turns golden. Add sesame seeds to the mixture.

Pour the mixture over the bananas. Drizzle lime juice and sprinkle lime zest over the bananas and serve.

A Chinese Food Celebration: Chinese New Year

Chinese New Year is celebrated by Chinese people all over the world. Also called the Spring Festival, it celebrates new beginnings and is a time for Chinese families around the world to get together, enjoy special food, and wish each other well for the coming year.

What Is Chinese New Year?

Chinese New Year marks the beginning of the new year according to the Chinese calendar, which follows a 12-year cycle with each year named after a different animal. The New Year falls in January or February on the second new moon after the shortest day of the year. Celebrations are held for up to 15 days!

How Is Chinese New Year Celebrated?

Chinese families prepare for the New Year by cleaning their houses thoroughly to get rid of bad luck. They also decorate their houses with red banners and even paint the doors and window frames red because red is a lucky color. On New Year's Day, everyone wears new clothes and gives presents, especially *hong bao*, which are red packets filled with "lucky money" to give children a good start to the year. Joyful parades with Chinese dragon and lion dances take place at the end of the two-week period, as well as fireworks displays.

Lion dancers may have to climb high while in costume so the lion can "eat" green vegetables hung in front of businesses.

During Chinese New Year, entire streets may be filled with red decorations.

Food

Many symbolic foods are eaten during the New Year, especially on New Year's Eve, when people travel long distances to celebrate with their families. Duck symbolizes faithfulness, a whole chicken symbolizes prosperity, tea eggs symbolize fertility, and garlic chives symbolize eternity. Desserts are symbolic too. Cakes represent a rich, sweet life and their round shape is a symbol of family reunions.

On the first day of the New Year, sticky cake is fed to the Chinese Kitchen God and, often, a vegetarian dish called "Buddha's Delight" is served, because no animal or fish should be killed on that day.

Lion Dances

During Chinese New Year, lion dance troupes visit homes and businesses. The lion dance is believed to bring good luck and good fortune.

Eating together during New Year celebrations is very important to Chinese families.

29

Try this!

Cooking is a creative skill you can enjoy every day. Try these activities and learn more about cooking Chinese food.

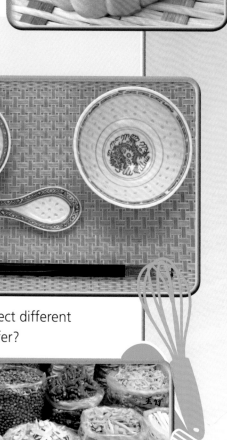

- Pick a Chinese festival, such as the Moon Festival, which is also known as the Lantern Festival. What special food is eaten during this festival? Try making it!

- Find your closest Chinese grocery store. Pay it a visit and buy an interesting ingredient to cook with. Perhaps some star anise or five-spice powder?

- Find out about Chinese pottery and how it has been used to display and store food, by visiting your local library and getting online. What is your favorite pattern?

- Collect different Chinese dishes to use when serving Chinese food. Think about which plates display certain food best, such as dumplings.

- Find out more about an early Chinese dynasty. What sort of food was served during this period? What food from that time do we still eat?

- Where in China does your favorite Chinese food come from? Collect different recipes for this food and compare them. Which recipe do you prefer?

- Make a list of spices commonly used in Chinese cooking. Create a scrapbook with pictures of these spices along with a list of recipes in which they are used.

- Visit a dim sum restaurant and find out as much as you can about the different dishes you enjoy. Where in China do they come from? What ingredients are in them?

Glossary

allergic
having an allergy, or a bad reaction to certain foods

Buddhist
a person who follows the religion of Buddhism

calories
units measuring the amount of energy food provides

carbohydrates
substances that provide the body with energy

civilization
the culture and way of life of a society or country during a period of time

climate
the general weather conditions of an area

culture
the ways of living that a group of people has developed over time

deltas
areas of low, flat land, often shaped like a fan, where a river branches out before flowing into the sea

diets
foods and drinks normally consumed by different people or groups of people

economy
the system of trade by which a country makes and uses its wealth

fertile
fruitful or capable of producing good crops

garnish
use a small amount of a certain food to add flavor or color to a dish

gluten
a protein found in wheat and some other grains that makes dough springy

Jews
people who follow the religion of Judaism

Muslims
people who follow the religion of Islam

native
living or growing naturally in a place

nutritious
providing nutrients, or nourishment

protein
a nutrient that helps bodies grow and heal

staple foods
foods that are eaten regularly and are the main parts of a diet

traditions
patterns of behavior handed down through generations

Index